From the Mist

From the Mist

SARAH AGNEW

RESOURCE *Publications* · Eugene, Oregon

FROM THE MIST

Copyright © 2025 Sarah Agnew. All rights reserved. Except for brief quotations in critical publications or reviews, no part of this book may be reproduced in any manner without prior written permission from the publisher. Write: Permissions, Wipf and Stock Publishers, 199 W. 8th Ave., Suite 3, Eugene, OR 97401.

Resource Publications
An Imprint of Wipf and Stock Publishers
199 W. 8th Ave., Suite 3
Eugene, OR 97401

www.wipfandstock.com

PAPERBACK ISBN: 979-8-3852-5075-2
HARDCOVER ISBN: 979-8-3852-5076-9
EBOOK ISBN: 979-8-3852-5077-6

VERSION NUMBER 052925

This one is for my niblings,
and the kookaburras.

Contents

Acknowledgments | 9

In the summer sunshine | 1
flight | 2
returning | 3
homing | 4
it was not peace | 5
at the breaking | 7
Forty | 9
After we said no | 10
Beauty in the mirror | 11
Together | 13
losing time | 14
Nine lives | 15
replanted | 17
In the warming air | 18
beyond death | 19
watershed | 20
Coffee with Dad | 21
had I been someone else | 22
The Yuletide Dinner Party | 23
of the instant goodbyes | 25
A stretch | 26
this mo(u)rning | 27
through streets I, only, know | 28

to hear your voice | 29
Too far away | 30
cocoon for a fatigued being | 31
Turning | 32
a spat with ghosts | 33
Very brave | 34
Poet's curse | 36
Beast of rage and fury | 37
Pierce the night | 38
hope arising | 39
on women's words | 41
Spiritual, but not | 42
New life begins in love | 44
with feathers | 46
Promise of warmth | 48
to cherish | 49
The seaweed is not brown | 50
in motion | 51
Dads are not sandcastles | 52
When all is said . . . | 53
waiting for rain | 54
Home, where the rain falls | 55

Acknowledgments

Poems in this collection previously published:

On sarahagnew.com.au: of ripples glistening; returning; to cherish (as 'cherished'); Together.

On Art/s and Theology Australia: replanted; Prayer of a wilting tree; in the warming air (https://artandtheology.net).

'Pierce the Night' and 'In the Summer Sunshine' first published in the e-book 'Hope is Coming', 2024, sarahagnew.com.au.

My thanks to creative communities convened at a workshop with Jude Aquilina for The Effective Living Centre, Wayville SA; UCA Women in Ministry Retreat, NSW; Rise Events, Canberra; Blackwood Uniting Church; Christ Church Uniting, Wayville; and my family and friends, with whom I have shared moments that have woven themselves into poems.

In the summer sunshine

after Christina Rosetti's "In the bleak midwinter"

In the summer sunshine,
dusty desert plains
shimmer red and ochre,
reach to bluest waves.
Long before your human birth,
Wisdom, here you were,
dreamed and dreaming,
long ago.

When we tell your story,
carol Christmas time,
whisper through our singing,
"All the Earth is mine.
"Stars that guided travellers,
sheep in the fields;
donkey and shepherds,
all in my embrace."

As we wait again, God,
wait with us we pray;
patient and impatient
for the peace you gave.
Peace is far from many hearts,
how we long to know;
in the bleak, or sunshine,
here and there and now.

flight

sunlight flicks the surface ripples,
glistens gold on dew-dropped leaves;
warms my legs and blinds me as I
squint past upper story windows
to the vast pristine blue

from hidden perches, kookaburras'
laughter draws joy from my heart,
plays it on my face—how I missed
this delight, their chuckling song

the heron gliding past
both mirrors and carries
my soul: they are my wing-tips
skimming lake's surface, it is my
beak turning toward the sun

returning

golden floodlight lifts greens
to bolder brightness against
deep grey—lifts me
on a rolling wave of petrichor

I can almost hear on my heart's
memory, the ocean—
a sudden taste of crisp granny
smith bursts through till my face
turns into renewal fresh
as mist from a waterfall

homing

Is it shelter, safety,
security after uncertainty,
these rented rooms and garden;
proximity to family, familiar
hills of childhood days?

Or is it the pigeon
coo-cooing, nestled
in branches above the clothesline
that pull my heart's
roots into home in
this hilltop suburb by happy
reservoir—cooing that carries
me home to the nest of kin,
to the dream of one day
living in Nanna's 1930s
bungalow two blocks
from the sea?

it was not peace

when I arrived, the sea
was not purring: she was
bubbling
        wave after
                    wave
onto the shore. I pushed
the big straw hat with
its yellow flower hard
over my ears and let my
bare feet feel the warm sand
all the way to the water
I craved,
       to walk
through the shallows
                    slowly
and breathe the salt air
                  deep—
to pray
       to listen
              to be

had I come for serene
lapping of ripples barely
grown enough into waves,
quiet still sunshine to hold
me in my troubles?

I stopped, sunk toes
and heels into wet sand,
facing now the clear horizon,
chin up slightly into sun
and let the wind buffet
me if it will

there was no revelation,
perhaps not even peace;
yet, although she looked
nothing like it today, the sea
held up a mirror
                for me
to see the strength I need
                        to be,
the stillness I seek,
and then to turn and walk
back, into the wind

at the breaking

every morning that I
am in time for stillness,
feet up, lean back and greet
the sun between hilltop
and veranda edge, I am
surprised again—the light on, or
seeming from, gums
rising from this valley I have called
home more years than I
have not; each return—
a resting from dream's pursuit,
or broken by its cost—
they are here; this spring
time of year, new leaves
shimmer fluorescent against
the settled olive eucalypts; new
leaves, new life on a breaking day
    (could it be that my life
    breaking could be making way
    for something new?)
heralded by kookaburras,
whose laughter's soon replaced
by screeching cockatoos,
my cough, a dog, and an engine
starting up to interrupt
their joyful song, but not
for long enough to chase
from me the hope as grey
clouds now chase away

the sunshine and the blue
to cast a muted tone to even
those brave shoots—for even in
the shadows there is light
enough; even in the rainclouds
there is life

Forty

40 days in wilderness
3 hours on a cross
24 hours of questions, torture
3 days in the abyss

40 days in wilderness
40 days alone
40 days tempted
An accuser, hunger, thirst

40 days in wilderness
12 years bleeding
40 years in wilderness
Lifetimes begging, blind, lame

40 days in wilderness
40 nights alone
40 days in company
Angels and self, beside

40 days in wilderness
Seconds under water
3 days in the abyss
through death, rebirth, life

After we said no

Oh Holy One,
we were so afraid
of what we did not know:
we were too afraid to try.

Oh Holy One,
are we so afraid
of one another?
Too afraid to love?

Oh Holy One,
we are so afraid
politicians will betray us again:
too afraid for trust.

Oh Holy One,
we've been so afraid:
we've let fear take the reins.
Will fear bring us undone?

Oh Holy One,
we may be afraid
now of the future we have created:
afraid enough to give up?

We cry to you.
We yearn for you.
Send your love
to quell our fear;
send peace, send hope,
don't leave us alone.

Beauty in the mirror

"Beauty will save the world":
written on a t-shirt from *Image Journal*

It is not beauty
that will save us—
it will be us;
it will be our choice
to see

the beauty in the face
of the Hamas soldier
aiming a gun at hostages;

the beauty in the face
of the hostage down
the barrel of the gun;

the beauty in the faces
of the children far away
from the finger on the button;

the beauty in the faces
of soldiers ordered to pull
triggers on faceless strangers;

the beauty in the faces
of the faithful in the mosque,
the synagogue, church, and temple;

the beauty in the face
of the other candidate
when meeting in debate;

the beauty in the face
of the woman you chose to love,
the lives you made together;

the beauty in the face
of the person in the mirror—
look.

Beauty will save the world
when we choose to see
the beauty here before us

beauty in the face of
beauty in the mirror

Together

When you speak, it is
to dream a healing
for us all, a rising
from the ash, the dust,
the death that's gone before;
you speak a gift, a
grace, a love to lead
us into life, to bring us
with you on your re-
emergence, make it *our*
re-emergence, though we've no
right to assume; and when
you speak, I want to hear,
to bid all to listen:
could you, our First
Peoples, be our Elders in
the Australia we could become?

losing time

we miss the good old days
when we could run,
when we had fun
in the thick and throng of it all

we miss the times
when we could walk,
it was us who talked
the talk we taught and trusted

we wish we had again
the way we knew back then;
the people we loved,
the roses and sunshine

we're lost over here now
books on shelves unopened
tea cups stacked behind glass
dusty and empty and cracked

we miss being held, and holding,
being heard, and hearing,
the song played as we knew it,
when we could keep the beat

Nine lives

I am like a cat,
or so, apparently,
it seems,
to understand
how to turn to land
with safety, when

I fall. Do cats have extra
courage? Lower fear,
of the edges,
                of hot tin,
of limbs that thin the further out
they venture; time
and time again hunting

a fall? To delve into dark
spaces, tight places; to trap
themselves away; and yet,
to also need the coaxing back,

to climb once more into the light
and breathe again? Do
cats trust in resurrection,
in life after, life beyond,
life even in the dying; in

rising, if not in landing
on their own four paws? Am
I like a cat, or less, in the trust
I place in the net
that will hold me when

I fall? I am not scared to face
the dogs, the rats, the cats
who stray into feral
ways—ears twitchy, fur
upright, tail flicks at attention;
tongue licks at tender
wounds in the safety of

the den. And you may see
softness, grown back over, but I
know where scars itch
and ache, and I may still
flinch when I allow you
close enough

to touch; venture out from the high
retreat, the long sleeps, the
cosy hide-away from which, again,

I rise.

replanted

after Psalm 1

dig in deeper
to the river
running living water
my roots dive for
depth strives for
after dusty shallows
rocky fallows deserted
so I'm thirsting
from the working hard
to stay alive
and now it's simple
to truly thrive
by the source
realigned with this replanting
though the uprooting
from familiar
mud dried up
shook the muck
from my feet and I
am replete
digging deeper
down
into
the river

In the warming air

a Psalm

Sun beams kiss the clouds white,
their linings silver on a cobalt
canvas, pull cotton strings
to float my sinking heart.

That's you all over, Creator,
isn't it? Bouncing balloons across
horizons to evoke delight from even
the gloomiest of days;

it's creation singing its silent
ode to you, is it not, turning
mourning cloths to dancing robes,
catching us all unawares.

It's your notes the bees hum
when humans lose the tune;
your melody the wind runs
wild and free with the geese:

lift our hearts with yours,
all you trees, and fields crowded
with flowers singing—bring
us home into the Song.

Geese are a Celtic symbol for the Holy Spirit.

beyond death

a dreamt silent stroll;
conscious, wagtails willing sight:
parenting for life

watershed

it is not only grief
for this aunt I'll not laugh
with again, that glint
of mischief returned to star
dust now; not the grief for Dad,
his glimmer gone before her;
it is not grief for all at
rest, not alone; nor is it only
a lament for the closeness
of kin; it is, too,
much frustration, pain,
fatigue, this post-exertion
malaise dragging on for days
and weeks; and it is the flick
of the tail, the beast kicking trauma
dregs up in my face
again, an editor's "no"
again, judge deciding not
again, life wearying over
and over

Coffee with Dad

his Liverpool mug
in my hands this liquid warmth
mocha, memories

had I been someone else

my closed eyes searching
for the hook you would
have dropped into my deep,
had grief not got in first;

I want again the tips
of fingers' touch as I handed
you a key to actual doors,
though we did not speak
the disappointment at the absence
of another you might have gently
turned had it been offered;

I fold my bottom lip
between teeth that could have bitten
lip or lobe or nape to playfully caress
as you stood half-dressed in my
kitchen on this side of a world
that quickly locked all gates
we could have opened . . .

The Yuletide Dinner Party

All manner of guests arrive
at Christmas, and I let
them in, listen to each in turn.

There's Christmas Past, of course,
all warm hugs and stories
of love and light and laughter.

Sneaking in after her is Guilt, who then
loudly notes the parcels under the tree,
my what STUFF you have, and what you do not give . . .

Relief as The Giver enters, Their
reminder of deeper riches, of
the part I play in a grander Story.

Until, here comes Lonely, its chest
pains and wistful flicks through
photos of the ones we miss . . .

Grief barrels in like a big
swell to dump me or drown
me—*look at the empty*

seat there, he cries, *and another
this year, and*—now warm
salty rivers flow

I flee to bathroom sanctuary—
the guests have made
themselves at home anyway.

I return when Joy arrives with hats,
balloons and bonbons
to burst with delight.

Some sort of balance, at last,
at the Yuletide table, and to each,
I turn and raise my glass.

of the instant goodbyes

click the red button leave
the red button end
for all

    and fall

        and fall

into chasm

        to a sudden
crash

    into lonely

        only
to climb for the start
again, but I cannot start again,
cannot launch for the heart's
wrenching again, for more
of that emotional

        upheaval

A stretch

The week together
hardly together
not alone
until
the last night
the eyes
the lean
the lips
before
the distance
stretched
again
and stretched further as I
awoke

this mo(u)rning

the driver behind me
for a moment looked
like you—
        I longed for us
to be, after all, heading
to the same place
              —oh
how we would embrace

through streets I, only, know

between sleep and waking / this morning / I was driving a car I could not make /
           accelerate /
                      not even with extra pedals / or holding them in my hands as I lay prostrate before the steering wheel / stuck in traffic on streets I only know / asleep / these roads a web of knots I / cannot /
           negotiate, all lost all stuck / until /
                                      I park / a street away and walk to my best friend's home / which suddenly resembles a house I lived in for a year / long ago /and as she declares that they / are going out tonight instead / I gather up my things all
        falling / out of bags / and arms / and try /
to find my way back

to hear your voice

We walked slowly together, you in a suit, briefcase in hand, me pushing a lawnmower over, on reflection, quite grassless terrain until I decided to stop, turn off the motor and turn back, walking slowly alone.

"I'm coming back, Dad," and you will switch the case to the other hand; I will hook my arm in yours and we will talk, as we walk. It's been four years.

Beside two houses, facing each other, newly built all on their own in dusty fields, I turned on a tap to wash my hands, but though I turned it off, water flowed, or seeped up, rather, through the earth of stacked books I stepped over, returning to you, still ahead, until I woke, yearning.

Too far away

When loneliness expands with aching
I dream of one too far to bring me comfort

When loneliness expands into the empty
I dream of one too far to fill the space

When loneliness expands beyond the bearing
I dream of one too far to help me carry

When loneliness expands my heart to yearning
I dream of one too far to live beside me

When loneliness expands towards a breaking
I dream of one too far for catching any pieces

When loneliness expands to fill my dreams
I dream of one too real for waking

cocoon for a fatigued being

hung on fairy lights,
copper beaded padding press,
thunder roll weaving

Turning

Lying still beneath the weighted
blanket and my eye wheat bag,
privilege is feeling joy,
awe and wonder, as thunder shakes
photo frames, and rain dances

on tiles; across town, friends
hold fear
       at bay as their daughter,
mother of a new, new,
grandchild, clings to life
again in a hospital bed;

elsewhere, others I know
receive diagnoses, prognoses,
the cancer cut out, and life
goes on a while longer.

So it is that I turn off the noise
and lights and lie in still,
silent gratitude, nothing
changing in my own life
of chronic pain, heavy fatigue, but this—
turning in to joy.

a spat with ghosts

for seven years my every day
was unencumbered by the ghosts
of dates I failed, but now I am
returned to this graveyard
of a love that scarce drew breath
and each afternoon constitutional
from my office down William's Road
(King of where and when, I forget)
I pass this tomb and find it is you
I want to tell that they
have ripped its guts out, the cosy booths
of seclusion I did not understand, the red,
the velvet, the curtains—I never understood—
the oysters, the Lover's Song, My Best Friend's
Wedding—one tomb, and all
the ghosts have gathered,
throwing me off balance

but I return their playful
jibes with a kiss for each,
blow the ghosts back home

and tomorrow, perhaps I will walk
the other side

Very brave

How I hope they see me

My Aunt is very brave

She stands in front of people,
can be quite silly as she plays.
My Aunt stands in front of lots of people
and speaks, and sings, and prays.
When we are born, get married,
and even when we die,
she has helpful words to say.

My Aunt is very brave

She's flown to far-off places,
all on her own.
My Aunt went where she
could learn, face challenges,
and grow: my Aunt asked for help,
instead of chasing dreams alone.

My Aunt is very brave

She is not afraid of needles.
My Aunt has four holes pierced
in each of her ears, a feather pen
and pretty flowers painted
right into her skin.
She did it all with a grin!

My Aunt is very brave

When people threw tomatoes,
smelly eggs and sticks and stones,
she stood tall
and let them fall.
My Aunt walked through them all,
and out the door to safety, friends, and home.

My Aunt is very brave

She says "No" a lot.
"No, I won't work more."
"No, I won't do all the things."
"No, it doesn't hurt too much,
I'm not too tired, yet."
"No. Now I have run out of gas,
can't play with you anymore."

My Aunt is very brave

My Aunt is not hiding.
She is resting.
My Aunt bravely naps,
she sits still doing nothing
but being where she is,
when all the world keeps
telling us to run and run and run.

My Aunt is very brave

Poet's curse

I imagine a hex
invoked over poets
at birth, so that,

although he asked me
to compose the words
for this national, pivotal
moment;

although they told me
thank you, again—in this
commemoration, my voice,
my presence, reassuring;

although I trust the Sacred
gift, Maker's invitation
to collaborate, generate,
create anew with Wisdom:

all I hear is a clatter
echoing in an empty
chasm as words tumble
from my heart.

Beast of rage and fury

Where is it hiding, then,
that beast of rage and fury?
Now I've caught its wretched scent
I am a hunter, in a measured hurry.

That beast of rage and fury
painted browns and greens: it tricked
this hunter. Now in a measured hurry
I sniff them out from under: the reds.

Painted browns and greens, it tricked
my eye to skipping past; but wakened,
I sniff them out from under, the reds:
I lift, I peel, I tear away at truth.

My eye, skipped past, now wakened
to the monster lurking deep within,
and I lift, I peel, I tear away at truth,
bleed freely, feel the scream at last.

To the monster lurking deep within
I look, now bared, now free;
I bleed, freely, feel the scream at last.
It is mine: the anger, it is me.

I look, now bared, now free,
no more hiding, then:
it is mine, the anger—it is me;
I, the hunted, I caught, I now spent.

Pierce the night

Sing to: "Silent Night", Franz Xavier Gruber

Rage through the night,
cry with your might.
Rage all night,
lift your cries.
Holy infant, what is this life?
Holy One, born into our strife.
Wisdom, God is with us,
foolish, Holy love.

Still of the night,
almost quiet;
sheep are fed,
all are tired.
Shepherds listen, all is well,
till the heavens burst, angels fall,
dazzle with holy song:
Jesus, hope is come!

Where is the peace
Earth still seeks?
Promise giv'n,
us to keep.
All creation labours and groans
for new life, for ease, for hope:
Wisdom, come, be with us,
help us truly love.

hope arising

hearing Michelle, Mikhaila, Alison, Jade, and Tania speak at the Rise Christmas Party 2021

from this still space,
this gentle pace of gather,
together, communion,
we ponder—hope—
hope that is cultivated,
we're captivated in its creativity,
connected in its love,
to its source in love,
in Holy, in Spirit, in
human, its energy,
your care, your carry;
hope is found in love.

and hope looks here
with honesty, it turns
towards my shadow,
embraces fear to look beyond—
hope leans into the ebbs
and flows, it opens vision,
deepens love, hope
welcomes change,
things do not stay
the same—and hope
is hard: it works, insists,
it is the grit of women
digging in together,
to the possibilities,

the creativity, this hope,
this tea to still us,
harp to soothe us,
lens to see us,
art to help us see
ourselves—for hope
is found in love.

hope will play
and hope will sing
and hope will bounce
with joy; hope will help us
fly with freedom from
these shadowed years,
will water seeds, will
shine like sunbeams,
and we will grow,
and we will flourish,
rising yet again.

on women's words

Jazzmeia spinning round
tiptoe vocal dance on dimes
tired eyes smile in time

treasures shimmer, shared
Miranda's invitation
a bruised spirit soothed

Katie swings, soars, sews
balloons and aerialists
how they fly, how we

Spiritual, but not

fragile
we call to each other
fragile
we meet
fragile
breaking, falling apart
fragile

we stand together
fragile strangers
fragile humans
more human
together, fragile
opening to Sacred
mystery, fragile breaking
falling open
fragile contesting
fragile ideas
fragile faith
breaking, falling out
of transcendence
wanting a falling into
transcendence

fragile claiming
Spirit—we are
Spirited—we are
storied, we are
fragile
feeling

faithful
freedom
to meet each other
meet with Mercy
find after death
fragile life

This poem was composed in response to a conversation at Uniting College for Leadership and Theology, facilitated by Andrew Root, exploring "ministry in a secular age", and the idea that the secular is not "a-religious" space to be filled by religious space, but a shared fragilisation of the varied beliefs, ideas, faiths, religions, philosophies to which humans shape our living.

New life begins in love

For Blackwood Uniting Church, Advent 2022

When new life begins,
it takes time to grow;
when a new life starts,
it needs time to know
what life it will be,
what shape and what colours;
it must learn how to find
what it needs to be nourished—

or does it somehow know
in its DNA, in its very being,
to reach out into the warmth
of the earth; by feeling,
seek water and food—
and look! it has already
begun to grow! Although
wobbly at first, before steadying

and strengthening, and lengthening;
uncurling roots down deeper,
legs and arms out further,
leaves and bodies, wings and feathers,
all sorts of life takes time to grow
from a seed away from the light,
reaching out with a knowing
to reach out towards life.

New life has its beginning
with the Spirit, Creator,
Wisdom inspiring all growing,
from galaxies to Earth's own Nature.
New life is made of
stardust and love—
yes, most of all, we begin,
and we grow on, in the mystery of Love!

with feathers

"hope is the thing with feathers"—Emily Dickinson

we celebrate the phoenix
risen from those ashes,
praise her vibrant feathers,
rapid growth again with force
we cannot fathom
                      and we avert
our gaze from her fiery
days, from the crimson fading
burgundy and brown; we will not watch
as the riches of her plumage shed
beauty from her perch,
as she shrivels—

look at her weakness!
at her pain as flames
engulf her: hope is *that*
ugly thing with feathers
burning, life dying if it is
to be reborn into
the flight she will excite
in us as she soars
and lifts our spirits
into life beyond
the faded,
the shed,
the death

and while others search for gold,
the ruby feathers of resurrection,
I—oh, how I—will hold
one scraggly, one scorched,
one faded feather of her dying
as I sit on my own perch
in tatters, waiting for the final
puff of smoke to signal life

Promise of warmth

kookaburra revelry
fills the dusk-dim valley

the moon and I keep watch,
remember friends keeping time

the sky and I take deep long breaths,
seek healing, seek rest

seasons overlap like clouds
that subdue the sunlight; summer

fevers rage, bodies shiver,
exposed post-hibernation

our muscles ache, and our bones,
my hand in my niece's, beneath her cheek

Winter's left overs
wash purple tears in torrents –

a brother, all of a sudden;
a mother, cancer let go at last.

While kookaburras fill the valleys with mirth,
jacarandas proclaim rebirth

to cherish

my body leans into it,
the warmth: starved of it,
these winter days of grey

my body reaches up to it,
the expanse: breathes again
out from under

my body stretches into both,
the descent, the climb:
relishes feeling strength

my body crouches down to it,
the mirror hardly rippling
its echo of a lone cloud today

my body whispers to it,
the Moreton Bay fig and its
thick, curving branches flung wide

The seaweed is not brown

But the waves do not hear
above their fussing, their rushing
to devour the beach once more,
so I slow down and tell myself:
That piece there, it's almost gold;
and the greens, like olives, grass,
and limes! over there it's drying
to grey in camouflage against
the sand, and here, it's dark
enough to be a purple, or maroon.

I could marvel at my seeing
colour today as if I never
have before—but perhaps you
know the feeling of emerging
from the mist?

in motion

Poetry is an eighteen-month-old in my arms,
resisting, resisting, then yielding;

a canopy of purple,
Jacarandas painting the streets;

a hopping Grey—stopped suddenly—
from its spotlight, turning all to ice;

the lilac and peach Squishmallow
hermit crab gift for my "Wee Hermitage";

chocolate—rich, dark, chocolate,
with a big South Australian Red;

my eight-year-old niece glittering
a wink across a crowded room;

the green I can smell after
the lawnmower cuts to silence;

a four-year-old "Spider Man" running
into his aunt's arms, full of stories.

Dads are not sandcastles

Dads are not sandcastles
Dads are teddy bears
Dads are squishy chairs
Dads are the home to which we return

Dads are not sandcastles
Dads are court jesters
Dads are DJs
Dads are laughter, long, long after

Dads are not sandcastles
Dads are tour guides
Dads are helicopter pilots
Dads are a houseboat on the River Murray

Dads are not sandcastles
Dads are sages
Dads are all ears
Dads are the wisdom we hold dear

When all is said . . .

I favour hugs over handshakes
I favour kind over cool
I favour spring or autumn—not summer any more
I favour jazz or baroque
I favour not listening to country or rap
I favour poetry
I favour meals cooked for me
a clean house, but not the cleaning
I favour dark chocolate
I favour a solitary life
I favour belonging in community
I favour a good story, well told
I favour silence
I favour family, and proximity again,
friends in person, though I'll take them, far
I favour cross stitch over embroidery;
walks at the beach, my feet sandy and wet;
watching lightning over the sea
I favour Austen
I favour Scotland
I favour Adelaide in the hills
I favour Shakespeare
I favour hugs over handshakes
I favour kind over cool
I favour close, enough
I favour poetry
and jazz

waiting for rain

not buried, planted
but longing—oh, how long
downfall heavenly

Home, where the rain falls

1.
I come from a land of thunder
storms and kookaburra calls.

2.
In a place of silent storms
and seagull caws of such variety,
each rare roll from sky to earth
brought me a moment of home.

3.
Home in a land of thunder stilled,
harsher sun and empty clouds,
seagulls carry me back
to the castle and crags that were,
briefly, for me, as they had been for
ancestors long, long ago.

www.ingramcontent.com/pod-product-compliance
Lightning Source LLC
Chambersburg PA
CBHW061247040426
42444CB00010B/2283